STATE PROFILES

VERMONT

BY COLLEEN SEXTON

BELLWETHER MEDIA • MINNEAPOLIS, MN

Blastoff! Discovery launches a new mission: reading to learn. Filled with facts and features, each book offers you an exciting new world to explore!

BLASTOFF! UNIVERSE

BLASTOFF! Beginners — GRADE K

BLASTOFF! READERS — GRADES 1-3

BLASTOFF! DISCOVERY — GRADE 4

This edition first published in 2022 by Bellwether Media, Inc.

No part of this publication may be reproduced in whole or in part without written permission of the publisher.
For information regarding permission, write to Bellwether Media, Inc.,
Attention: Permissions Department,
6012 Blue Circle Drive, Minnetonka, MN 55343.

Library of Congress Cataloging-in-Publication Data

Names: Sexton, Colleen A., 1967- author.
Title: Vermont / by Colleen Sexton.
Description: Minneapolis, MN : Bellwether Media, Inc., 2022. |
   Series: Blastoff! Discovery: State profiles | Includes bibliographical
   references and index. | Audience: Ages 7-13 | Audience: Grades
   4-6 | Summary: "Engaging images accompany information about
   Vermont. The combination of high-interest subject matter and
   narrative text is intended for students in grades 3 through 8"–
   Provided by publisher.
Identifiers: LCCN 2021020864 (print) | LCCN 2021020865 (ebook)
   | ISBN 9781644873519 (library binding) |
   ISBN 9781648341946 (ebook)
Subjects: LCSH: Vermont–Juvenile literature.
Classification: LCC F49.3 .S48 2022 (print) | LCC F49.3 (ebook) |
   DDC 974.3–dc23
LC record available at https://lccn.loc.gov/2021020864
LC ebook record available at https://lccn.loc.gov/2021020865

Editor: Rebecca Sabelko   Designer: Andrea Schneider

Printed in the United States of America, North Mankato, MN.

TABLE OF CONTENTS

LITTLE GRAND CANYON

Quechee Gorge is more than 1 mile (1.6 kilometers) long and 165 feet (50 meters) deep. It is known as Vermont's Little Grand Canyon.

It is a warm fall day in Vermont. Hikers stand on a bridge high above the Quechee **Gorge**. They hear the Ottauquechee River rumble as it flows far below. They take in the bright colors of the surrounding forest-covered hills.

OTTAUQUECHEE RIVER

OTHER TOP SITES

BEN & JERRY'S ICE CREAM FACTORY

ROCK OF AGES GRANITE QUARRY

SHELBURNE MUSEUM

SMUGGLERS' NOTCH

The hikers head to the bottom of the gorge. They follow a wide dirt trail under the shade of tall trees. Canada geese honk overhead. The trail becomes steeper. The sound of rushing water grows louder. The hikers reach the river's edge. They wade in and splash in the cool water. Welcome to Vermont!

WHERE IS VERMONT?

Vermont lies in **New England**. This region covers the northeastern United States. Canada is Vermont's neighbor to the north. The Connecticut River forms Vermont's eastern border with New Hampshire. Massachusetts lies to the south. Vermont shares its western boundary with New York. Lake Champlain stretches for about 120 miles (193 kilometers) along this border.

Vermont is a small and narrow state that covers 9,616 square miles (24,905 square kilometers). The capital city of Montpelier sits near the middle of the state. The largest cities lie in northwestern Vermont. They include Burlington, Essex, South Burlington, and Colchester.

NEW YORK

N W E S

6

CANADA

LAKE CHAMPLAIN

COLCHESTER

ESSEX

SOUTH BURLINGTON

BURLINGTON

MONTPELIER

CONNECTICUT RIVER

VERMONT

RUTLAND

NEW HAMPSHIRE

A GREEN STATE

Vermont's name comes from the French words *vert* and *mont*. It means "green mountain." Vermont's nickname is the Green Mountain State.

BENNINGTON

MASSACHUSETTS

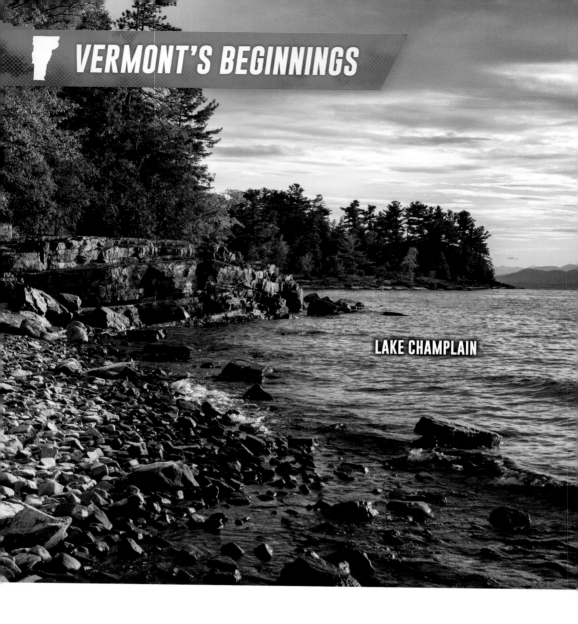

LAKE CHAMPLAIN

People arrived in Vermont about 12,000 years ago. Native American tribes formed over time. The Abenaki, Mahican, and Pennacook lived in **wigwam** villages. Explorers reached Lake Champlain in 1609. They claimed the region for France.

The French established Fort Sainte Anne in 1666. The fort protected fur-trading routes in the northeast. In 1724, the English built Fort Dummer in the southeast. England battled with France and gained all of Vermont by 1763. In 1777, Vermont declared its independence and formed its own government. Vermont fought alongside the 13 **colonies** in the **Revolutionary War**. After the war, it became the 14th state.

NATIVE PEOPLES OF VERMONT

There are no federally recognized tribes in Vermont, though some Native Americans live in the state.

WESTERN ABENAKI INDIANS

- Original lands in New Hampshire and Vermont
- Vermont recognizes four Abenaki tribes

PENNACOOK INDIANS

- Original lands in Vermont and parts of Maine, Massachusetts, and New Hampshire
- Some descendants live in Québec, Canada, today
- Also called Pawtucket and Merrimack

MAHICAN INDIANS

- Original lands in parts of Vermont, New York, Massachusetts, and Connecticut
- Some descendants live in Oklahoma and Wisconsin today
- Also called Mohican

Vermont is a land of mountains and valleys. **Granite** peaks rise in Vermont's northeastern corner. Lowlands line much of the Connecticut River. They slope up in the west toward the Green Mountains that run through the middle of the state. In the northwest, the Champlain Valley's lowlands border Lake Champlain. Islands dot the lake. Fast-flowing streams cut through the Taconic Range in Vermont's southwest.

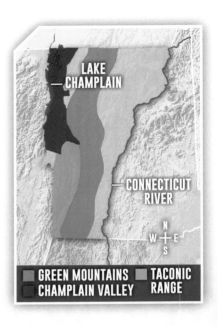

LAKE CHAMPLAIN

CONNECTICUT RIVER

N W+E S

GREEN MOUNTAINS   TACONIC RANGE
CHAMPLAIN VALLEY

CONNECTICUT RIVER

GREEN MOUNTAINS

SPRING
HIGH: 54°F (12°C)
LOW: 34°F (1°C)

SUMMER
HIGH: 78°F (26°C)
LOW: 58°F (14°C)

FALL
HIGH: 56°F (13°C)
LOW: 40°F (4°C)

WINTER
HIGH: 29°F (-2°C)
LOW: 12°F (-11°C)

°F = degrees Fahrenheit
°C = degrees Celsius

VERMONT'S CHALLENGE: AN UPTICK IN TICKS

In Vermont, ticks are active more days each year as temperatures rise due to climate change. Tick bites can spread diseases to people. The diseases used to be rare. In recent years, hundreds of cases have been reported in the state.

Vermont's short summers are mild and rainy. Winters are long and cold. Temperatures often dip below freezing. More than 120 inches (305 centimeters) of snow piles up in the mountains each winter.

Vermont's forests are full of wildlife. Black bears scramble up trees to grab fruits and nuts. Moose seek the forest's cool shade in hot weather. Eastern bobcats stalk squirrels, rabbits, and deer. Gray foxes leave their dens at night to hunt mice and small birds. Woodchucks **burrow** in fields at forest edges.

In meadows, hermit thrushes peck the ground for insects. Red-tailed hawks soar overhead. Honeybees sip nectar from buttercups, violets, and goldenrod. Beavers build dams in rivers and streams where trout and salmon swim. Turtles, frogs, and salamanders live in Vermont's wetlands.

BLACK BEAR

GRAY FOX

HONEYBEE

MIDLAND PAINTED TURTLE

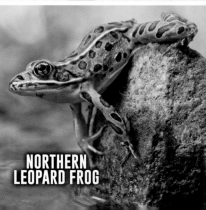
NORTHERN LEOPARD FROG

12

HERMIT THRUSH

Life Span: about 9 years
Status: least concern

hermit thrush range = ▮

LEAST CONCERN	NEAR THREATENED	VULNERABLE	ENDANGERED	CRITICALLY ENDANGERED	EXTINCT IN THE WILD	EXTINCT

13

Around 643,000 people live in Vermont. It has one of the lowest populations in the country. More than three out of five Vermonters live in **rural** areas. Their farms and small towns dot valleys throughout the state.

MONTPELIER

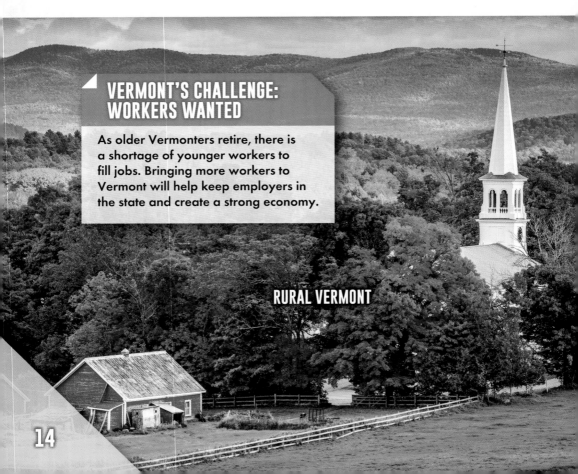

VERMONT'S CHALLENGE: WORKERS WANTED

As older Vermonters retire, there is a shortage of younger workers to fill jobs. Bringing more workers to Vermont will help keep employers in the state and create a strong economy.

RURAL VERMONT

FAMOUS VERMONTERS

BEN COHEN   JERRY GREENFIELD

Name: Ben Cohen
Born: March 18, 1951
Name: Jerry Greenfield
Born: March 14, 1951
Hometown: Burlington, Vermont
Famous For: Creating Ben & Jerry's ice cream company, which is known for Chunky Monkey, Cherry Garcia, and other wacky flavors, as well as for doing charitable work around the world

More than 9 out of 10 Vermonters have European **ancestors**. Many are **descendants** of English, Irish, and French-Canadian **immigrants**. Small numbers of Black or African Americans, Asian Americans, Hispanic Americans, and Native Americans live in the state. Newcomers have arrived from Canada, Nepal, Jamaica, and the Philippines.

LAKE CHAMPLAIN

Founded in 1763, Burlington drew **settlers** to work in its sawmill and shipbuilding businesses. The city had become an important lumber port by the mid-1800s. Today, Burlington is Vermont's largest city and center of industry.

POWER UP!

In 2014, Burlington became the country's first city to run totally on renewable energy. Wind, sun, and water are important energy sources used to produce the city's electricity.

Burlington sits on a hill overlooking Lake Champlain. Residents enjoy sunset views from Waterfront Park. They relax at nearby beaches. Bikers pedal the popular Burlington Greenway along the lake's shoreline. Church Street Marketplace features shops and restaurants. In summer, residents go there to dine outdoors and listen to street musicians. The South End neighborhood's many galleries make it a center for the arts.

INDUSTRY

LOGGING

Logging drew many of Vermont's early settlers. Today, forests cover much of the state, and logging remains an important industry. About one in three Vermont factories process harvested wood into products such as paper, furniture, and hockey sticks. Other factories produce computer and machine parts. Miners cut slabs of granite and marble in Vermont's **quarries**.

A SWEET SPOT

Vermont is famous for its maple syrup. In 2020, Vermonters made more than 2 million gallons (7.6 million liters). That is about half of all the maple syrup produced in the United States!

Many of Vermont's farmers raise dairy cows. The milk they produce is turned into cheese and ice cream. Apples and corn are grown in the Champlain Valley. **Tourism** is a big business. Resorts and hotels employ workers who serve visitors. Other Vermonters have **service jobs** in schools, banks, and hospitals.

DAIRY COWS

INVENTED IN VERMONT

INTERNAL-COMBUSTION ENGINE
Date Invented: 1826
Inventor: Samuel Morey

PLATFORM SCALE
Date Invented: 1830
Inventor: Thaddeus Fairbanks

SPOON FISHING LURE
Date Invented: 1834
Inventor: Julio Buel

MODERN SNOWBOARD
Date Invented: 1977
Inventor: Jake Burton Carpenter

GRILLED
VENISON

Vermonters enjoy hearty, local food. **Traditional**
wild-game suppers feature grilled **venison**, black bear
stew, and raccoon pie. Corn chowder and lamb stew
are popular on cold winter days. Cooks add butter and
lemon to **fiddleheads**. Cheddar cheese is a favorite
among a variety of local cheeses. Apples from local
orchards fill apple pies and flavor cider donuts.

Maple syrup features in classic dishes like maple baked beans and maple cream pie. Maple creemees are a popular ice cream treat. Sugar on snow is a winter tradition. Vermonters drizzle boiled maple syrup on fresh snow. They eat the cooled and hardened syrup.

FIDDLEHEADS

SUGAR ON SNOW

MAPLE APPLE CRISP

8 SERVINGS

Have an adult help you make this sweet treat!

INGREDIENTS

5 medium apples
1/4 cup maple syrup
1/2 cup all-purpose flour
1/2 cup rolled oats

1/2 cup brown sugar
1 pinch salt
1/2 cup butter, softened

DIRECTIONS

1. Preheat the oven to 375 degrees Fahrenheit (190 degrees Celsius).

2. Peel, core, and slice the apples. Place the sliced apples in an 8 x 8 baking dish.

3. Pour the maple syrup evenly over the apple slices.

4. In a bowl, mix together the flour, oats, sugar, and salt. Cut the butter into the mixture until it is crumbly.

5. Sprinkle the mixture evenly over the apple slices.

4. Bake for 35 minutes until the topping is golden brown.

5. Serve warm or at room temperature.

SPORTS AND ENTERTAINMENT

SUGARBUSH
SKI AREA

When winter arrives, Vermonters head outdoors. They go snowmobiling, snowshoeing, and ice skating. Skiers and snowboarders hit the snowy slopes. Residents celebrate spring's arrival at sugarhouses. They turn sap into maple syrup.

A MONSTER MASCOT

The Vermont Lake Monsters team mascot is Champ. Legends state that Champ lives in Lake Champlain. Since 1609, there have been more than 400 reported sightings of Champ in the lake.

When the weather is warm, Vermont's lakes draw swimmers, boaters, and fishers. Audiences enjoy summer theater performances throughout the state. Baseball fans cheer for the Vermont Lake Monsters. Many communities host craft fairs and antique shows. Residents also relax at cafés and shop at local **farmers markets**. Fall is a great time for hikers to explore the Long Trail in the Green Mountains.

LONG TRAIL

NOTABLE SPORTS TEAM

Vermont Lake Monsters
Sport: Futures Collegiate Baseball League
Started: 1994
Place of Play: Centennial Field in Burlington

CENTENNIAL FIELD

Vermonters enjoy the Brattleboro Winter Carnival in February. They join in games, ski races, and sleigh rides. June's Quechee Hot Air Balloon Festival draws crowds from across the region. Festivalgoers enjoy balloon rides high in the sky. Food and live music entertain people on the ground.

The Vermont State Fair takes place each August in Rutland. Livestock shows, musical performances, and more bring Vermonters together to celebrate summer. The town of South Hero hosts its Apple Festival each October. A petting zoo, cider pressing contests, and other activities honor the annual harvest. There is so much to see and do in Vermont!

SOUTH HERO APPLE FESTIVAL

QUECHEE HOT AIR
BALLOON FESTIVAL

1609
Explorer Samuel de Champlain claims Vermont for France

1770
Vermonter Ethan Allen forms a group called the Green Mountain Boys to keep New Yorkers from taking their land

1791
Vermont becomes the 14th state

1666
France establishes Fort Sainte Anne on Lake Champlain

1775
Vermont joins the 13 colonies to fight in the Revolutionary War

1923

Vermont native Calvin
Coolidge becomes the
30th U.S. president

2011

Vermont experiences
serious flooding after
Hurricane Irene strikes

1970

Vermont passes the
Environmental Control
Law to protect the
state's land and wildlife

1881

Vermont native
Chester A. Arthur
becomes the 21st
U.S. president

2019

Senator Bernie Sanders
of Vermont runs for
president

VERMONT FACTS

Nickname: The Green Mountain State

Motto: Freedom and Unity

Date of Statehood: March 4, 1791 (the 14th state)

Capital City: Montpelier ★

Other Major Cities: Burlington, Essex, South Burlington, Colchester, Rutland, Bennington

Area: 9,616 square miles (24,908 square kilometers); Vermont is the 45th largest state.

Population
643,077
(2020)

STATE FLAG

Adopted in 1923, Vermont's flag features the state's coat of arms on a blue background. A pine tree on the coat of arms represents the state's forests. A cow and bundles of wheat stand for agriculture. The Green Mountains are in the background. A deer's head atop the coat of arms represents Vermont's wildlife. The state's name and motto appear on a red banner below the coat of arms.

INDUSTRY

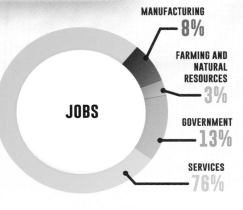

MANUFACTURING
8%

FARMING AND NATURAL RESOURCES
3%

JOBS

GOVERNMENT
13%

SERVICES
76%

Main Exports

paper

machine parts

electronic parts

aircraft parts

Natural Resources
soil, forests, granite, marble, slate, talc

GOVERNMENT

Federal Government

1 REPRESENTATIVE | **2** SENATORS

VT

3 ELECTORAL VOTES

USA

State Government

150 REPRESENTATIVES | **30** SENATORS

STATE SYMBOLS

STATE BIRD
HERMIT THRUSH

STATE ANIMAL
MORGAN HORSE

STATE FLOWER
RED CLOVER

STATE TREE
SUGAR MAPLE

GLOSSARY

ancestors—relatives who lived long ago

burrow—to make a hole or tunnel in the ground by digging

colonies—distant territories which are under the control of another nation

descendants—people related to a person or group of people who lived at an earlier time

farmers markets—markets where local farmers sell goods

fiddleheads—young ferns that are curled at the top

gorge—a narrow canyon with steep walls

granite—a hard, textured stone used for building

immigrants—people who move to a new country

New England—an area in the northeastern United States that includes Maine, New Hampshire, Vermont, Massachusetts, Rhode Island, and Connecticut

orchards—areas where fruit or nut trees are grown

quarries—large open pits from which rock and other materials are dug

Revolutionary War—the war from 1775 to 1783 in which the United States fought for independence from Great Britain

rural—related to the countryside

service jobs—jobs that perform tasks for people or businesses

settlers—people who move to live in a new, undeveloped region

tourism—the business of people traveling to visit other places

traditional—related to customs, ideas, or beliefs handed down from one generation to the next

venison—meat from a deer

wigwam—a dome-shaped home made with bark or animal skins covering a structure of wooden poles

AT THE LIBRARY

Ades, Audrey. *Ethan Allen and the Green Mountain Boys*. Hallandale, Fla.: Mitchell Lane Publishers, 2018.

Hackett, Jennifer. *Vermont*. North Mankato, Minn.: Children's Press, 2019.

Krull, Kathleen. *A Kids' Guide to the American Revolution*. New York, N.Y.: Harper, 2018.

ON THE WEB

FACTSURFER

Factsurfer.com gives you a safe, fun way to find more information.

1. Go to www.factsurfer.com.

2. Enter "Vermont" into the search box and click 🔍.

3. Select your book cover to see a list of related content.

INDEX